How to use this book

Follow the advice, in italics, given for teachers on each page.
Praise *the children at every step!*

Detailed guidance is provided in the Read Write Inc. Phonics Handbook

8 reading activities

Children:
- *Practise reading the speed sounds.*
- *Read the green and red words for the story.*
- *Listen as you read the introduction.*
- *Discuss the vocabulary check with you.*
- *Read the story.*
- *Re-read the story and discuss the 'questions to talk about'.*
- *Re-read the story with fluency and expression.*
- *Practise reading the speed words.*

Speed sounds

Consonants *Say the pure sounds (do not add 'uh').*

f	l	m	n	r	s	v	z s	sh	th	ng nk

b	c k ck	d	g	h	j	p	qu	t	w	x	y	ch

ar

Vowels *Say the sounds in and out of order.*

short   long

at	hen	in	on	up	day	see	high	blow	zoo
					$\bar{a}$	$\bar{e}$	$\bar{i}$	$\bar{o}$	$\bar{u}$

a i e
u

*Each box contains one sound but sometimes more than one grapheme. Focus graphemes are **circled**.*

Green words

Read in Fred Talk (sounds).

cat   wi<u>th</u>   bla<u>ck</u>   <u>th</u>in   fi<u>sh</u>   frog   clap   lo<u>ng</u>

si<u>ng</u>   pup   pen   and

Read the root word first and then with the ending.

jump   →   jumpi<u>ng</u>

Red words

<u>th</u>e   <u>y</u>our

Vocabulary check

Discuss the meaning (as used in the story) after the children have read each word.

definition:

lap   *a place to sit on your legs (fish in your lap)*

On the bus

Introduction

Have you ever travelled on a bus?
What did you like about sitting on a bus?
What did you do?

In this story there are some very strange looking animals travelling on the bus. There's a fox and a cat, a dog and a frog, a pig and a hen, and they are all wearing very funny clothes!

Clap clap clap

Story written by Gill Munton
Illustrated by Tim Archbold

Sit with us
on the big red bus
with the fat black cat
and the fox in a hat

Sing with us

on the big red bus

with the long thin dog

and the jumping frog

La la la la

Clap with us
on the big red bus
with the fat red hen
and the pup with a pen Clap clap clap

Clap clap clap

12

Sit, sing and clap
with a fish in your lap!

Questions to talk about

FIND IT QUESTIONS

✓ Turn to the page

✓ Read the question to the children

✓ Find the answer

Page 10-11:   Who sings on the big red bus?

Page 12-13:   Who claps on the big red bus?

Page 12-13:   What do you have to do with a fish on your lap?

Which words would you use to describe this bus?

(funny, weird, silly, peculiar)